# On the Margins
of Great Housing Estates

Also by Andrew Duncan

Poetry
*In a German Hotel*
*Cut Memories and False Commands*
*Sound Surface*
*Alien Skies*
*Switching and Main Exchange* *
*Pauper Estate* *
*Anxiety Before Entering a Room. New and selected poems*
*Surveillance and Compliance*
*Skeleton Looking at Chinese Pictures*
*The Imaginary in Geometry*
*Savage Survivals (amid modern suavity)* *
*Threads of Iron* *
*In Five Eyes* *
*Radio Vortex* (ed. Norbert Lange — translated into German)
*On the Margins of Great Empires — Selected Poems* *
*With Feathers on Glass* *

Criticism
*The Poetry Scene in the Nineties* (internet only)
*Centre and Periphery in Modern British Poetry* **
*The Failure of Conservatism in Modern British Poetry* **
*Origins of the Underground*
*The Council of Heresy* *
*The Long 1950s* *
*A Poetry Boom 1990–2010* *
*Fulfilling the Silent Rules* *
*Nothing is being suppressed* *
*Beautiful Feelings of Sensitive People* *

As editor
*Don't Start Me Talking* (with Tim Allen)
Joseph Macleod: *Cyclic Serial Zeniths from the Flux*
Joseph Macleod: *A Drinan Trilogy: The Cove / The Men of the Rocks / Script from Norway* (with James Fountain)
*Rustbelt Arcadia* (with John Goodby)


* original Shearsman titles
** revised second editions from Shearsman

# On the Margins
# of Great Housing Estates

Andrew Duncan

Shearsman Books

First published in the United Kingdom in 2025 by
Shearsman Books Ltd
PO Box 4239
Swindon
SN3 9FN

Shearsman Books Ltd Registered Office
30–31 St. James Place, Mangotsfield, Bristol BS16 9JB
*(this address not for correspondence)*

EU AUTHORISED REPRESENTATIVE:
Lightning Source France, 1 Av. Johannes Gutenberg, 78310 Maurepas, France
Email: compliance@lightningsource.fr

ISBN 978-1-84861-996-8

Copyright © 2025 by Andrew Duncan
The right of Andrew Duncan to be identified as the author of this work has been asserted by him in accordance with the Copyrights, Designs and Patents Act of 1988.
All rights reserved.

# CONTENTS

The History of Shopping
    (a) Llyn Cerrig Bach      9
    (b) The Goths as inventors of tourism      11
    (c) Equidistant      12
    (d) Shopping for Books      13
    (e) One absolutely perfect cultural object      17
CCTV Underground      19
Fragment 355M/636k/12      21
The Dumb Book      24
Who owns the river      25
William Hallam Pegg      28
The Brig at Torthorwald      31
Nottingham Alabaster (and some gypsum)      34
Low-resolution      36
Capistranus Triumphans      39
Under Controlled Conditions      43

Calendar Rite
    X1 The Cold River      47
    X2 Thematic      48
    X3 Coloured Dust      49
    X4 Performance Fear      50
    X5 Banal Poem About Fallen Leaves      52
    X6 Performance High 1      53
    X7 Performance High 2:
        *A Romance of the Docks*      54
    X8 Gnosis      56
    X9 Carrion Crows      58
    X10 A Route March in the Cultural Field      60
    X11 The Cologne Mani Codex      62
    X12 Non counterpart      64
    X13 Inside and Out      65
    X14 Dissident      67
    A Cold River 2      69

| | |
|---|---|
| AA Calendar Rite | 71 |
| Y14 Poem of gofyn and diolch, being of request and thanks for a gift | 74 |
| Y13 Outside and In | 77 |
| Y12 Gnarls and Snibs | 80 |
| Y11 The Origin of Space | 82 |
| Y10 The Catalogue of Ships | 83 |
| Y9 Carrion Crows Stay Up Late | 85 |
| Y8 In a River | 87 |
| Y7 Performance High 3: Sparse Terrestrial Rim | 88 |
| Y6 Performance High 4: Altyn-Dagh | 90 |
| Y5 Jealousy | 92 |
| Y4 The North Circular Motorway at Silver Street | 93 |
| Y3 Theme with Loss of Variation | 94 |
| Y2 Coloured Dust 2 | 96 |
| Y1 Cold River 3 | 97 |
| Notes | 98 |

*On the margins of great housing estates*

The green lights of the village gush out from the teeming mouths of wheat, sunflower, and sunn, wild apples, tender ripe onions, green belladonna, cloves, and buckwheat, cascading like cascades of water down a throat of ripe and fallacious apples.
　　—computer generated text (*GPT-2*)

# THE HISTORY OF SHOPPING

'Only the prisoner shall be free, only the poor shall be rich, only the weak strong, only the humble exalted, only the empty filled, only nothing shall be something'.

## (a) Llyn Cerrig Bach

This is the lake where an Iron Age deposit of metal artefacts seems to result from the Celtic preoccupation with bodies of water as a site for ritual deposition – an arm of the boundless where payment could be made to the gods for the benefactions of past and future harvests, perhaps. Virtually, these are the swords from which the famous sword came, that was handed to Arthur out of a lake at Avalon.

One of the objects is a fetter – the first, we are told, ever to be found in Britain. Its conformation does not suit a cow or a dog. It is suitable only for confining a living human body. Glimpse of a social order, lapping around the class era like an ocean, where there were no slaves. Of a shining society, without differentiation, moving like the sea, sliding over itself and back. Approach of the Mediterranean. Run-up of a society with awesome powers for producing prestige goods, alluring a simpler society, with no money and few specialists, into stern measures for a counter-prestation. It must have been the nobles of the tribes who nominated the genealogically marginal as slaves. This is – we know it – a first step in the history of shopping. Britain enters the Mediterranean economy as a satellite, a blank page – exporting raw materials, war-dogs, and its own inhabitants, as slaves. The arrival of a range of goods, from overseas, with more tiers of rank, destabilises the old order. The social system convulses and turns into a form with more niches, where differentiation means that political freedom is an attainment; there are nether niches where people are simply unfree. The higher civilisations are more expert in devices of confinement, indoctrination, debt, and torture. The tribes cease to be the complete image of a cosmos, held in place by analogies, and start to be the world periphery, their lands and humans signed with a perceived inadequacy of ownership.

The vast deposits of finely wrought metal, invisible but fiercely imagined as gleaming, in the rivers, lakes, or hanging from splendid trees in the groves or *nemeta*, already represented a mighty expense and self-raising: the objects which support the words one utters to the gods. The upward thrust of assimilation is now diverted to a new task: of shopping. Ports are built so that the ships of Continental traders can approach with their fabled and heady cargoes. So that people with no appreciation of preciosity can become a commodity.

The vote of the owned is to have a home. The home of the owned is the extent of loss. What the owned know is a deficit economy. The admiration of the commodity is the cultured lord; white markless hands; a gaze where the high falls on the low.

## (b) The Goths as Inventors of Tourism

The long route of famine, breaking what they could not carry –
Just an old clatter of pots and pans. Accumulation is what you leave.
Possession straight from *session*, you sit down to enjoy it.
Blowing through thin pastures they devastate,
The long route of hunger. Of shadow series, the flocking delirium
Of what you couldn't have, dream treasures.
Herds multiply flesh wealth
And count down when the grazing cannot carry.
Eurasian fluctuation belt, this dirt is your dirt.
Bags and cans from the economy of shipwreck.

Driving through that fable
'Insatiable', lost in a cycle, at tip of a barren strip after
the herd had eaten down what could be bitten.
A wolf as guide.
Discarding what would not fit into horse-packs,
appetites intact. A market without funds.
Leaving little trace. The grasses regroup.

On the curve of the progress zone
They dig holes in the ground, empty pits
Of earth for firing, inventing the house.
Pits build up to production sheds,
Rows of warehouses and spoil heaps.
The real series of commodities, climbing vector.
The southern cities are depots for all wares.
Wealth gradient
Is no barrier ridge.
Dark periphery full of yearning.

Cycle terminator
In breach of boundaries.
A marine incursion like a shipwreck,

The shores depressing under its weight,
The poor people of Europe in flood
Surfing behind a boat. A line of shields
Dragging the moon out of place.
A northern displacement.
Guided by a flock of carrion birds, auspices,
A commodity gradient shuttles the poor
Into the shopping centres of Gaul and Italy.
The Empire drawing in new forces,
Lose your voice and face. But you love yourself.
At latest with Alaric
The invention of tourism:
Classical cities
Recontextualised by off the scale designers.
They didn't want those Baltic beaches and the strand-grass
So we had to go to them.

I was a barbarian unclear I wasn't a god,
We spotted a vacant empire with original features,
Aromatic and wine-rich. We flew there in the company
Of cranes. A fuselage of yearning.
How close can you get to blue perfection
Without it being turned on by you?

An erasure at the origin of states.
*Spear rise spear fall*
*Sortes Gothicae*, dice you throw to win
The casino, the showgirls, the police chief
And the land division.
You say trailer trash, I say Russian roulette.
Cast a thousand lots, risk and thrill.
The land registry is a sprawl of notes,
The smiles of fortune, fallen leaves of the first book:
*Origo Gothica.*

Honour-avid eorls turfed new earth
Dire-drenched drengs statuted serfdom.

The most booty is in temples and cities.
Turn the herds into straps and bags.
Forget about carrying the shopping home,
We buy the hotel.
*A deposit of the self*
*That solves transport problems*
And moves the problem families to a new town.

It was like that film, you know,
*Parade armour for a dying gladiator.* Gold crows
That treat the rich like a delicatessen. It was Sunday
And we sacrificed the losers. Thought of all the things we don't own
And took half. Weighted on a perfect point,
Acuity turning, then wipe peel off the blade. Half
Of what you ever wanted.
You offered me diamonds, fur coats, and champagne
As if sanctifying them. Can I get a witness?
Can I own a beach? Can I choke a crow?
Get this mosaic featuring me
Popping tags on an Istrian marble quarry!
Those jewellery boutiques were right where we stacked arms
And showered. That's not very *sophisticated*.

We say hi! to the world of objects,
Snare criminal dreams
And write their clauses out as a law-code.
The barbarian equity
Is that you are what you own.
The culture of the unschooled has it
That you can make names up for anything you steal.
Show me who used to own this city
And I'll show you my new poetry tutor.
Tear up my tab
I don't want the oinochoe
I want the vineyard.

## (c) Equidistant

A point is dissolved out of connections and is equidistant from all other points. It vanishes in a sky full of points, where every step is as likely as every other and no cell escapes from the constant grey.
A large library offers this boundless free variation reproduced at the level of articulated and finished trains of signals. The larger and more thorough the library is, the more it corresponds to stochastic noise on a monumental scale. The freedom sharply reduces as we choose a single book, which is why this step is so hard to take. Perhaps it is an error, a kind of falling to the ground. Not a word I heard could I relate. When everything we desire is at hand, we have to decide what to desire. The sight of completeness tells us that curiosity is a form of incompleteness: by devouring partial forms, we acquire an appetite for the data which completes those forms, and which is closely specified by the parameters of the incomplete form.

Why go through these metabolic burns to achieve the goal of tranquillity? At this point hurry enters the frame. We incite this state of incompleteness, tension, partiality, fallenness, in order to regain the sense of completeness. The data remains the same, but we enter a dynamic process with respect to it; like other appetites, prone to disorder and compulsiveness. Routes of rapid decay obscure classic and static forms.

Who could lock the gates by which we enter an incomplete state? The solution of asymmetry, where we move through least-energy states, processing nothing. Like the algae on the rock in the river cellar. Who could break the lenses and make the world of signals too faint to recover? Jochmann wrote his *Retreats of Poetry*, three thousand years of falling silent like a harmonic curve realised in wood, its smooth and lawlike decline. Once we knew we were gods we ceased to be gods.

Where a lens is a flaw and a mirror is a fall. A point is perfection and is equidistant from all other points. It vanishes in a sky full of identical points, boundless. A self scattered across this sky has no features and no flaws. It has ejected its organs. It is serial like number. It responds to no signals and dissolves into itself.

## [d] Shopping for Books

On the 27th of September 2003 I took the train to Cambridge to visit the university library. My list of books to borrow was: Will-Erich Peuckert, *Pansophia*. The *Straeon* of Glasynys, stories of the 1840s, described by Parry as faithful retellings of Welsh folk tales, free from the inflation of Welsh prose which took place in the Victorian era. A volume of the *Transactions* of the Gaelic Society of Inverness, the learned society dealing with the antiquities of the Highlands, to be used by me as a source of prose in Gaelic, to practice on and to extend my vocabulary. CW von Sydow's *Vor folketro*, our folk's beliefs, an account of folk religion in Sweden, part of a series called *Norden* which described the whole of Scandinavian folk culture.

As my enemies would have predicted, the library had none of these books. They have the TGSI, but you can't borrow those volumes. My whole project, so carefully planned and fantasized about in odd moments of quiet in the office, or just after waking up in the morning, had to be abandoned. I had to improvise and find interesting books by scent – the worst trail of all in a library with several million books.

Hands that scrabble through a bed of mud as if counting coins, pawing and pushing away and grabbing. I catch at an unlimited display of books, as if falling past them. Each is available, each is frustrating. I imagine the result of reading each one, as a good prudent consumer: a momentary image flashes on my brain. I start to get fever, my throat is sore, perhaps a small asthma attack. The brain fever sees whatever it wants to see. The images get more and more sketchy, overheated, overpowering, evanescent. I am listening to music at 100 times the right tempo. I only want things which are irretrievable, unreported, obscure, in little-known languages, ignorant of the main lines of European culture, marginal, exotic, irrational. And that is how I wanted to be myself. I implore von Sydow to have written the book I want to read. I am wildly over-excited, tired, unable to respond, everything now is disappointing. I can almost hear wires crackle and burn out. Such is shopping.

Culture, who needs it? None of the books here is a close match to what I desire. But perhaps what I want is in the next aisle? I couldn't bear to leave it on the shelf and be excluded just because it was in a language I couldn't read. No, I couldn't even figure out the title – that's even more unfair.

The shape of what I desire is specific – it mirrors the shape of my body. Its site changes constantly – cooling and heating up all the time like the air around my body. I own the desire I built and which was not fulfilled, and I own the frustration, a hot bag full of something unnamed. I move through the middle of an *Ich-Gestein*, an ego-geology, a landscape where all the parts run into me and I flow out into all the parts.

The fallback was to borrow five books – three in Welsh, one in Norwegian (from the Norsk Folkeminnelag), one in English about Hungarian folk customs.

The country houses of the land-owning families who formed the apex of society were full of collections of objects; and still are, with the families mostly gone or decollected. The rules of collecting allow for completeness and define future acquisitions – missing points of a series. As the middle class acquires leisure, it seeks to re-enact the successes of the gentry, and so culture becomes an act of collecting: in my case, of experiences rather than objects. The collection reflects the childhood predilections of its maker – in my case, folklore and linguistics, and being in the North. Acquiring culture in this format is a prestation, an act of conspicuous consumption which is not even visible – but virtualised, internalised. The poem is a collection of rare experiences and sets of words – a unique thing in a modest home, mimicking the fabulous treasures in the big house. The modern poem is like that other display possession of the gentry – the Folly. I write the book in order for someone to collect it.

I woke up on a boat on the Thames. It was light and no-one else was awake. Near my head was a book on Occultism and Alchemy, belonging to the owner of the boat, stuffed with hundreds of coloured illustrations of mystical events of transformation, of marriage, of the birth of worlds. It exactly matched Peuckert's book – according to a description I have, "He gives a historical sketch of the white and black magic of that time, the years of Faust and Paracelsus, of the kabbalistic movement, of the mysticism connected with the names of Ficino, Weigel, and Jakob Boehme. *Pansophie* shows us an intellectual world, which had fallen into oblivion for more than two hundred years(.)" I wanted to fall into that oblivion and become what it knew. Gazing over the deck, I could see the fabled reaches of Wandsworth.

## [e] One Absolutely Perfect Cultural Object

The core is accepting strangers, and the coveted objects,
The core is repetition and fixed order.
On offer, in matching colours, a stone wrist-bracer,
Microliths, bronze mirror, peat-bog,
Collection *Critique*, animal heads, industrial skips,
Coffee sops and blood-crusted wires.

Quiver of ibex leather and hazel wands,
Bronze dagger and stone bracer on wrist
Of lord for whom the sunbeam strikes as nimbus
Tooling strap details in a splash of colours and fine fabrics.
Modularised for export to a thousand sites.
Wear the set and enter the story.

The horse is waiting for a rider, the continent
Is all recorded as tenures, on skins. You get the seat for
A romance in which high status males and females
Cycle through love and warfare without a climax,
Cells reproducing across variant geology.
Feathered hermits and arrogant enchantresses,
Miracle, fealty, and passage of arms
By the Tarn Wathelyn in Inglewood Forest.

The ticket says you're Steve Bannon for a day.
It was depthy. Even *smelt* like the pipe cracking heads
Outside the neighbourhood bar where the guys watch the HUAC show.
Shatter post-doctrinal half-truths, empathemes. Opencast brains
Crackling like frayed flexes of 1953. *Live* the
Blue-collar geopolitical re-enactor, his
3-word ideologemes beaming in over infected earpiece.

I was drafted for the Blair-era Grand Project
To mitigate the effect of society on social life.
Do you have faith in them? Can you read their quiet signs?
We were soaring in the service of others,

I got into the legend and out of the curve,
They used my press release to sop up coffee,
*I got kicked out of the Social Exclusion Unit.*

You go to a mall with many zones
To pick up the thing you have lost.
We peak in the Perfect Zone
But could not remain.
You love the thing you want
You frequent a café where you used to have it

In the *grande surface* we got the book through the till,
And in the Café Pique on the next level down
We were Connected and not touching the ground.
*Editions de Minuit.* Exclusivity opened up –
The core is accepting strangers,
And lit me with its nimbus. We had the refrains,
Those great lines were meant for us.
Gilles, Félix, and me. Collected the set.
One foot on the Left Bank
And one on the shore of the Trent.

In the poverty-owning cosmocracy
Every identity is temporary and replays from system start.
In the strict regime of abundance
A sense of self comes free with the purchase.
You catch the recursion and take home
One absolutely perfect cultural object.

# CCTV UNDERGROUND

The house sailing on a sea of rain
Gathers soot and silt to funnel down
The pipe fixed to the wall
Into the dense root-plait choking the way

The jasmine tapped the six feet of pulsing black silt
Its roots got thirsty on the drain
A brush of roots swept water inwards.
Swelled to the bore of the clearance channel
Which backed up, in a bubbling spring.

Blue bricks of the back yard lifted and stacked
As the hidden emerges into shot
On a screen on wheels. A yellow plastic frame defends it.
A cable with camera at its tip
Is sailing bravely into the darkness of the drain
A diode light pinned to its forehead.

The jasmine, breathing
It does so catch water in a net
A hand without a palm
whose fingers drink straight through the skin
Drinking and binding in refinement of greed
It strikes the deepest roots, the narrowest and most fined down clutch,
The most competitive and penetrating, whipping its holes as fine as
                                                        [water-seeps,
drafting the subsoil into an organ of jasmine.
Tripping up houses from the toe
A message of me
Sprayed upward cascade of nutrients.

The earth arches its back;
The tip detaches and swims off, through layers of black humus
The fine world of roots, the cells of larvae,

Acid and humus and mineral seeps
The waterways sliding towards day.
Drawn down sightless channels with the run-off
Sailed through 100 lightless colours.
An eye hidden in its own horizon
Lashed by curiosity, a spasm of nerves
Glimpsing sleeping couches of broken stone.
Where the soil is milled,
Where the brooks gather, where the rain is drowned,
Dissolution is a night without dreams
Leaching by laws of the slope down from the archaic crags.
The royal barque of the pristine eye
Comes forth by day
Bearing a strip of knowledge
Traced by a star in the upper darkness
Commanded by symmetry.

# FRAGMENT 355M/636K/12

Even as it becomes a tree,
Or a rose by water.
The seed is like the rose petals,
They are fragrant air which calls down the flowers.
Roses attempt now to cover the room,
But in the reflection basin
They too will burn up in the light.

The rose by water drops is called, Riccardo Tissante.
The rose by water droplets is named, Capriccio Taranto.
The rose by water drops is called, Isotta Ticino.

The rose by water droplets is crowned, Riccardo Avola.
The rose losing water drops is withered, its petals fall

Cherish the wine and pine resin,
The memory of childhood and innocence.
Let not a chaste maiden despise
The suave investment analyst;
For him I return with more power,
With orders to preserve the integrity of the family,
With directions to inscribe the most abstruse meaning in the most circumscribed space.

Inevitably,
The whole triumvirate arises to oppose you.
They construct a meetings diary
To overcome you. You are too weak to parry them.
Triumphal sun, moons of summer above Tuscany.
How false are your dreams that I shall be greater than they are!
How false are your words that I shall be wiser than they are!
In Dorset the memory of your youth floods the brainstem,

In the Venice of the Long Island hills the Brunelles escort you to their
                                                                  [musical precincts.
In a silk quilt with embroidered cloth and moleskin,
You go into the little parlour where
The ladies shop, ornamented with racks of objects copied from abroad.
You attempt to emulate the carriage of the actresses,
You carry the ladies' clothes.

You go into the little parlour where
The lasses sing, and such attractive drawn faces are
Passionately surveyed through the nostalgia of the spectator.
You make the ladies' clothes.
As you go into the dressing-room, the lasses reproach you,
And envy your requirements, you fall to working under the guidance of men.

The mill-girls throw lots for dance partners.
As you go into the mills of the city
You see a hundred different dresses at once,
You make the catalogue of clothes for the different days of the week.
And the catalogue says,
You shall be a hundred different women,
Each one a different shape, each one a different brilliancy.
Each face a different affair,
In each hand a different wiping-cloth.

You shall be a hundred stories tall, weaving
Trees and bridges and reflection basins,
Each one a different brand of sap.
You shall behold a thousand stars,
Bridges of flesh with hundreds of ways
Open up over the plain of stories.
The viewing-glass sees the fifty-seven pathways of the self,
In the forty-three rooms of the same building.

You shall be a river and I shall be a beam,
We descend together like the rays of perfection,
Our torrents merging and effaced one by one,

The genius of the intellect mingling with the taints of the learned journals.
You shall behold seventy-one eyes and the wings of men
Crawling in the pile of dissolved light.
The genius of the machine shears and renders neat
The dawnlike grey of the clerical yellow flowers.

You shall swallow the world with hunger, and in that state
You shall not even taste the real food,
Because the packaging is lost in transit.
You shall sow a great grave and there shall be no crop.
You shall betray packaging with live flesh,
And become a god different from the auditors of Taste.
You shall mock the letters of the T-shirt
And imitate the voice of
Nature in the singing of birds.
You shall devour the world with a new outrage.

You shall possess whole souls and be conscious of nothing.
You shall labour for an eternity and see the clearly posted limits.
You shall see birds fluttering their feathers,
And in the end
You shall possess whole organs and see the bird in human flesh again.

You shall mock the orders of the older art and practice the new rites.
You will laugh at the older generation and their poems about walking.

# THE DUMB BOOK

An leabhar balbh, the dumb book,
Said by someone who possessed it then
To have been written by Seamas Mac Fhir Bhisigh
Maybe around 1560.
This book is lost.

Maybe the book of lost things,
The Book dumb while other books speak
How could it be a book with no voice?
A collection of things that can't be said
A *leabhar* of things that can't be said any more.

Maybe a list of things that had no voice
of pages that could never speak again
Of truths that could be known but not said
Of people whose voices did not carry far.

Of things that could not be remembered after time away.

To fill the calfskin with a tally of landless heritors
set out those who had not paid for finished eulogies
trace the holdings of the groundless
and find the black ink turning back to white

A writer to the dumbness
Of families that ceased to exist
And lands that disappeared from under them
Due to improvements to the law.

The patrons resolved that which would be forgotten.
Seamas, from a family of scribes and genealogists,
In Sligo.
*Firbissius, Firbissy, Forbès.*

## WHO OWNS THE RIVER

Property is vision
That you try to make strangers share.
Who owns the river? Who owns the dirt in the river? Who owns the
[fairway?

One perfectly happy village.
Chelsea Harbour, the houseboats lined up along the pontoon
Dry twice a day, south of King's Road
The ideal drop-out community scooping up ideal drop-outs
Creative, eccentric, chatty, sociable
Like a basket of kittens. Everyone hanging out
All the time. There is nowhere
I would rather be. This where
Is being drowned. Everybody doing fine.
Under fogbanks of music.
The boat stops being a home if they take the mooring away.
He is stealing your river. But who owns the river?

The owner of the water
By virtue of owning language
Which the water rebuts line by line
With its voices

A dock of rotten timbers half sliding back
Into water. Old crates and empty bottles. Peasants
Stumping through dirt. Natives of the mud. And water circling, a basket
[of river.

Citizens delegate the law to an assembly
which relegates it to landowners to exercise as sovereignty.
The government of the river
Is a profit-making company
Invested by law

And protected by secrecy.
The owner of the water taking the moorings away.
The law is equable between cruelty and kindness.
On the water you have no rights, as in music.
This was your home until someone richer wanted it.
Fatal swirls by the piers of the bridge,
Capital dissolved by clever arguments, re-framing.

Tidal ledge where westward water turns east,
The sea giving up its wishes
In the calm that ripples
Over the stakes of the old fish weir.

Old reaches of an ever new river
where a painter out of craziness upped anchor
and took his barge to open waters
Halfway to Holland, half to the river bed and its holes.
New moon draws the crabs, demersal flat stage
Draws a colour line across the North Sea, smudging
the Medway channel down
the unknown reaches past Chelsea Bridge
Effaces the coastline in gestural crankiness.
Malarial foreshore and thunderous tonalities.

Nature is a mirror for your wishes
and the Thames reflects when the tide and outward current reach a tie, still
point, glass estate of self-knowledge
From which no river can exit without turning into pure gold
Scales of its puzzling identity: what is eternally replaced
Never admits to change.

Soft shores of Bohemia
Where everything I say is true
And years pass like days
Metal spirals on a lost shield, agalma
In symmetry that defies grasp
Immersed to balance human and divine
Volutes like a forest drawn by instruments from silver.

Pigboats modelling the ego of a rich man
like modelling a heart in wax. Smeared candle.
Capsize. Squeeze the water out of the river.
Cormorant on the piling shakes its head
To get the fish lengthways into its gullet –
This fish can fly. Last species of a dead river turning back at the port of souls,
Lending its bed to geese and roach

Boiling up flints from the wrack line
& making those hunched vertebrae walk.
Paint faces in blue flint,
the knuckles and bones of a relationship
made to walk the ooze of the river.
Join these shanks into a boat
starboard and kingpost
cormorant and mitten crab
warped to clasp itself and be a vessel
embraced by bitter waters.

The river
Is big and cold
The river
Has the city as its offspring, its pool of spawn, the river
Forces its vermin down their throat
You are less live than this
Belly of living grey matter.
The river
Washes away in moments, and runs on.
Property is wherever humans can be hurt
Modernity means being evicted from your home.
The river
Warms itself on human bodies.

# WILLIAM HALLAM PEGG

It is 1934 and our man
Designs a picture of abundance, grace, and wickedness
Exposing, how the breakthrough was written down. The share prices
                                               [all went up
but Roosevelt didn't want the commitment
the bankers, the commissars, and the diplomats
all knew what was going to keep the world fed
and all settled inside their own position.
Pegg was using the medium of lace to make the truth visible
As it appears in Nottingham and to a designer.

Rendered in the machine-twisted medium
The skeleton of famine
And 60 buildings showing the world
And the commodities it produces in each part.
The octopus on the pergola
Is the money interest. The burning building
Is the temple of Mammon.
The fruits of the earth
passed through the channels of the sea
reduced to warehouses
or burning off, in lieu of marketing.
Do we need something soft and warm? We have wool
do you need something warming and alcoholic? We have wine
do you need something sticky and semi-solid? We have dates or toffee
do you need solid sunlight? We have shiploads of apricots

There is a squid on the pergola.
Why is the top register full of bats?

Eight bridges
Show the conquest of obstacle by engineers
And the passing of trade without stint.

Wooden bridges that crossed streams, swam away in winter.
Rivers broken by piers curl, turbine, swallow
Themselves. Turn, fail to flow. Gnaw. Bridges that hang from chains,
that are fixed by pylons
Curves that are realised in steel, broken descent paths
Sea bridges. footings firm against infirm waters.
Routes in the sky. Carrying vehicles. Carrying foodstuffs, stellages of
[barrels.

We remarked a shipwreck.
Warships have foundered and merchantmen in the bays close to havens,
They run aground in the shallows round the headlands, on the silt
[deposits
from the rivers.
The barrels of fish are packed with salt, a second voyage.
The abundance of each land
Is trusted to the embracing waters
And shared with each other land
The grapes taut with juice
Are crushed beneath milling arms of wood and spill their load
Into vats, ready for the vintage

We will provide lace in considerable amounts.
The programme is drawn in squares
The square reduced to movements of the needles
The series turned into an instruction card
Weaving jacquard lace without human hand
Hundreds of metres of fabric, rolling off and piling up and filling the mill
floor, billowing up
Towards the roof and its vast panes of sky.

He sets down the principal buildings of the contributing lands
The Parthenon, the pyramids, a castle, a pagoda.
The way of polychrome tiles
And the flat roofs to sleep on in summer
Gazing at calligraphic stars
The mud building that grows from a clay pot

Wrapping an empty space in a skin
That traps air and coolness
The basilicas with their balanced and humane façades
The fortresses with the falls of their curtain walls.
The captain sets his course. Across great waters he keeps the vessel safe.

# THE BRIG AT TORTHORWALD

In 1715
my grandfather's grandfather's grandfather's grandfather
being the pastor at Torthorwald
*in verbo divino praedicando praepotens ac mellifluus*
led out his parishioners to stop the Catholic army
of James III, needing the local brig
to be on its godless way.
So a few dozen men laid in wait for many thousands.
The mind must become what it beholds,
servant to each sense the skin is stitched with,
if you can't maintain order in your own parish
you have to admit a corrupt universe;
and consequently
you must stand off these royal armies.
Or should the gap in the cosmic defence,
the tear in the skin where the blowflies linger and copulate,
be the parish of Torthorwald?

Look, such soot from the Roman darkness
come here in frogged coats and tricornes
to twirl and blow and overcast a Scottish heaven.
Righteousness is not a wing of cavalry
nor is truth a country of great estates.
They cannot pass through this parish
whether flying troops of kerns in bratt and line,
vagrants from the rain house with fingers for every pin, or
regiments in European order, drilled and ranked.
Bred in the house of lies to make war for money
they carry seeds, wrapped up and cherished in a casket, of
an order where poor men are held to be of weak mind, as
courtiers and casuists prink in silks:
like England bloody, and more slaughterous
like England false, and more treacherous.

This same James kept court being countryless.
I beat them small as the dust of the earth
I stamped them like the mire of the street
And spread them abroad.

In Scotland by ancient liberty
divinity falls from the air onto the fields
to be gathered by the common people
as sheep do grass or the mouse scurrying up a hollow path.
Where the digger of ditches and dragger of stones
has a right of call of what judges make his law
or what priests utter the speech of God on the Lord's day;
or what thieves lift his sheep;
and is right to be led by those inward stirrings
where what the carnal eyes cannot take in,
lighter than a feather, finer than darkness,
the Holy Ghost brings,
and stows the body full of it as a salmon with leaping, an
effectual calling
the pure man hears once and does not flinch thenceforth.
Truth cannot exist
except in men.

Here where righteousness is dragged through the streets on hooks
like the animals that give up their breath in the gutter
the rich hissing of lies overlays that voice.

I am able-bodied
But my enemies are still alive.

Now the Spring gale has cut through their fountain
the petals of the magnolia tree
lie on the lawn in drifts like fallen music,
I look for traces in the sodden pink and white of
force, but find no intervals or edges.
Strewn neither evenly nor predictably
neither remembering nor asserting;

no message can be read here, no boundaries
suggest events or the curse of intentionality.
The eye searches for pattern and finds *Indifferenz*.

Should I denounce the errors of the States
or refute the claims of the Churches?
I float on the sweet inane fitful breeze,
grow wet when the rain falls, rot where it stands.
depolarised, unheightened, unmoved.
I lie down where I find support,
sink away where the slope draws.
Not contrasting or detoning
not possessing or contending
I moulder down as the locality intends.
The tumid clots discharge,
the clean sheer edges and colours fade
Nemesis returns all things to their places
I make myself thin and flexible.

By the time you find out who to fight
they're already paying you a weekly wage.

# NOTTINGHAM ALABASTER (AND SOME GYPSUM)

The ground fleeing underfoot or, rural
infrastructure in surface collapse
foundered and slipping down holes left by gypsum dissolution
along the seams, along the bands
part of the Trent's curving and swathing

traced and hacked out at Chellaston and Aston Glebe
columns interspersed with glacial drift
mass boles freighted in boats to Nottingham Wharf.

The trade of alabaster figurines
cheap designs for a cheaper marble, lustrous and part translucent.
The photo has restorers adding such gilding and gauding.
– garish like figureheads, like inn-signs, like strolling players.
Dead white Virgin doll. Still from a mystery play,
sacred scenes as shaped by a baker.

Blunt shapes forerunning
awkward conversations and lumpish speeches
dogma of the illiterate in fistfuls
flash-bang kitsch bumping along the bottom of its pond
ideas do not favour pictures.

Smashed in the 1530s in the cause of abstraction
forfeiting things to reach some inner life
in pieces where they stood
buried at Flawford in pursuit of heresy
defaced and defeatured, devils driven out of them.

Elsewhere my favourite waggonsful of solid smoke
from coal-fired power stations,
fly-ash caught in flue becomes flake gypsum
exalted ashes, earth's white adornment plaster
ready for painting.

gypsum seams as threads dissolving in rich groundwater
emptying a raft of air-sacs under Derbyshire
and pouring out down-dip with the run-off
dreamlike and dissolute

## LOW-RESOLUTION

I wake because the cat has occupied the hot water bottle
and I feel cold. A patch of warmth is close by
and a defeatured light has poured into the room
pale fell of an animal turning slowly like the sky
archive of a million dove feathers
and there are no objects at all.

Cold, twilight, exhaustion
the screen of consciousness is faint and drained out
attenuated in the geometry of darkness
the eye surrenders its heat
the spectator has left the theatre
camera/ drain
metabolic whose transforms are narrative
abandons hero and succession
to core bleed-out, flat arcs
*eye/ ejector*

a pale TV I can't switch off. tapes from the 50s
that get thinner and more blurred
the vortex of the black and white film
reeling on, reeling off
with cheap tales of love and crime
with blowsy footage of expense and prestige

burning has as pair a flare
where shapes dissolve in the cold to
clear new ash
this long lasting task
of echoing the world
and hitting it to raise a sound
has run its course.
the sheet light with its lack of colours
has receptors for the silent layers of the mind

a depatterned landscape
with its resources for deprogramming

Thin light excites
blank processes of a peripheral self
eventless field with its drain through
which light seeps
and sinks into the earth as drops tracing pores
the buried water reflects nothing
an archive with no memories
retrievals pulling up an isotropic edgeless hiss

where the featureless folds into the boundless
is the figure infinitely symmetrical or without symmetry?
does it contain all shapes or none?

there is a negative
of that sharp and edged moment
that would turn awareness on
like a flash of light
the loss of edges exposes
what is neither liquid nor vapour
neither black nor white
neither feather nor air
neither self or not-self
neither real nor nothing

a matrix with strips of unused cells
can map the greater range of the uncoded
as a set that stands for unused strips of sound
the silent series that surround language
ageless twilight unsnared by shape
a zone of patches not yet objects

they reflect a low-difference distribution
of, say, Iron Age domestic pots not exhibiting shifts
of social status or foreign invasion

over hundreds of years, retaining heat, or water
but not acts of prestige and show.
Just a million hollows.

the heat wiping out of you loses form
a cloak of feathers
a sparse body of bent air traces the self
swearing fealty and reciting
finds its own periphery.
How big is a feeling?
loss of signal 30" out into the room
you paper yourself with vapour
an outward curve traps
the breakdown of information
and epistemology has won.
Do I acquire poems to project that inside, its
thermal smear locked against dissipation? a cocoon shut
out of the series of time?

Zenith towers irradiate
rotating blades engage and dispel the twilight
there will be hot coffee and a visible world
The blank sheet
divides up into squares of equal size
to trace the recession of things into their sites
the optical tide
arrives in colours of different area
to pick up grains and boundaries
the lost intact shapes join up with a gasp
the grey sighs and dissipates
renouncing its dim and marginal identity

## CAPISTRANUS TRIUMPHANS
1456
*Machometes superbia elatus omnino conabatur subjugare Imperio Hungariam*

The field army of Mehmet II,
having destroyed the empire of the Greeks
and all armies that did not run away, sat
in three echelons around Christian Belgrade, in hundreds
of swift boats along the Danube. Experts
assessed this was the end of Europe and of Christendom. Investors
took that as a basis for calculations.
He moved along the Thiess speaking in the market places

some were Hungarian, some Czech,
the air was like an epidemic or the smoke from burning.
He spoke in Latin to a Magyar audience yet
the words lifted and carried them away,
the crowd dropped their trades and joined the banner
ready for captivity or death.
The sound was like a flock of birds killing each other.
Capistranus raised them with words
like a net raising fish out of the sea.

The audience moved south like a flood, or a panic of animals,
moved by a fever of the earth towards
the main Turkish army, waiting in
siege lines around Belgrade.

The question, always, is how language
mediates hysteria, how the sermons were in Latin
and the audience could not speak it. The madness of crowds, or,
the divine breath
moving from mouth to mouth
sweeping people into blind rages and fits of mania –
the loss of conscious control, drills
rattling themselves into fragments.
As further south towns

were under siege for months
expecting deliverance, or, massacre,
Mehmet II acquiring to destroy, as if a feast
to be wreckage the next morning. Ostrovitza,
Novo Brdo. Males killed off,
women and children haled to slave-markets, inflecting
prices by their mere abundance. The story piercing
to all points north, each town
waiting for the siege-train to arrive,
for its own investment. Transcendence
comes to those in fear of death, of loss of social being, of
final domination. *Slaves and
the mothers and fathers of slaves.*

A hole tears in reality. Silver-tongued Capistrano
director of pogroms
burner of many Hussites
keeper of heresy, lord of rhetoric
twirler of syllables, sees fire rising from human flesh.
*fanatic talking in tongues.*
The great sermons were physical and oratorical feats,
the apex of a culture. The voicing of the eternal,
chaining a crowd. *Hysteric and mime
A crow for John Goose.* Illiterates
attached to the abstract, to all knowledge ever known.
Perhaps minor friars, among them
translated headings of the sermon to the few nearest them.
Perhaps the panic was already there, waiting only
for a signal of release, an already dreamed of
rush towards danger.

The holy army marched to raise the siege of Belgrade
towards the Turkish veterans in their siege lines,
their galleys plying the Danube, the
conquerors of Constantinople
the irresistible.

Towards an army of all nations, chosen for their special services
for their bred-in way of killing or taking ground
Circassian light horse
Italian cannon masters
Venetian mariners
expat contractors knowing the *secrets of nature.*
Their high and incomprehensible banners
signing the different dignities of the Turks,

their engines of war
carried on camels, buffalo, and oxen
with vehicles of bronze, iron, and wood
and sonorous instruments in great number
the delivery of hard power

As pipes for conducting fire
*pixides sclopetos et spingardas*
of clarified metal charged with prismatic powder.
Lifted in crucibles
for the overthrow of cities.
River boats taken apart to carry on horseback,
reassembled in field workshops.
While the gentry of the kingdom chose not to fight
staying at home with their retainers and their stables –
horse lords, the substance of the cavalry
the volunteers
untrained and without officers
rustics, diggers, ploughmen
without supplies or horses
bearing clubs, swords, slings, iron hooks
the illiterate and inexpert
walk south caught in bliss of rhetoric
unable to move from column into line.

Once you believe that the miracle story is your story
you are deaf and can only see strange lights in the sky,
news of destined events reaches you without words,
the earth grows thin beneath your feet.

The Turks had broken down the walls and filled the ditches,
having entered the city by boat from the water-gates
the Christians fought on the walls of the citadel,
strewing the glacis with straw, fascines, and poles,
they thinned the attackers with fire
who fell back to the third line, to the heavy weapons stations,
then burnt the siege train and began moving south
towards Macedonia. Capistranus forbade any pursuit
being without cavalry, the expertise of nobles,
drawing his disciples off back to Hungary.

The irregulars dispersed back to their homes
the war was won
the lift of words dispersed
like a storm dispersing into small feathers of sound.

A door opens and people walk through it as a mass
towards a shared illusion. Senses beaten by excess of signal,
carried by a language they did not understand.
Immersed in the fantasies of collectives
like a flock of starlings scared by fire in the sky,
they hand over their fate to the legend,
they walk through the fiery furnace, soar
eighty feet up in the air,
march to the outskirts of Stalingrad.

# UNDER CONTROLLED CONDITIONS (MAY, 1981)

The black star falls.
First to the pub, waiting for the nerves to soak up the rich sap. An instant of time and space is photographed, a slab of brick and light reinforced and recorded, turned on its side for reconfiguration.

The first symptom is an access of politeness. Group dynamics sculpt themselves with pictorial clarity.

I see my thoughts like a blue liquid in the stem of a flower, foaming, rising and falling. There are a thousand flowers in the field.

It is no longer possible to have emotions. The animal is all surpassed…I can't see anything but plans, connections, arguments, dynamics. I don't want to do the things I do by day. Fields divided into two for argument merge in a higher group logic, the explosion of the self unstrings every sentence stored under the headword "I".

Every word links to ten others, every bud becomes a spray, every drop of thought refracts. My memory has never been so clear. I never perceived a room as space before. Only an insight can bring the shape inside you, through the bone wall. The room full of rolls of film is tumbling into the room, the camera has multiplied its power, the coloured sequences flow at will. The single perspective is lost. I chew but I can't swallow because I can't stop tasting. I suffer hallucinations of the lungs and calves. I look at a TV screen and see a different image from what the others are seeing.

Dolokhov asks me, as a mathematician, whether the deepest language of the brain is a series of pictures from which a set of mathematical relationships can then be measured or if it works in bursts of transmitted numerals of which pictures, decoding ratios like the receiver of a cable TV, are representations. I say, there are only two states of number: enough and not enough. Quantity comes from the stomach, the original digit space; which can measure the relative value of a pound of grain and an ounce of meat; which can even memorize places.

He says, mathematics starts from relations between groups, not quantity at all. He asks, what were the pictures from which the ten numerals were stylized.

A lizard crawls from his eye socket, looks around with a languid expression, and crawls back in. It is thought. A lizard darts into my foot and comes out of my eye as though I were a rotten tree. The ducts of my nerves are alive with lizards. I am completely helpless. The only parts of me that can move are lizards. I see on the wall the caduceus or herald's wand with twin serpents writhing up it. Satan, dialectic, the dragon flickering from level to level of the fixed real world; the Salamander, living not in flame but in the immobile material world.

Two reps or clawed lizards I once saw in a hangover slither out of an oubliette and into Dolokhov's ankle.

Then comes the Chinese phase.

Thought's just a liquid like blood scent, nectar, spawn in a pond. Words come out of my inner environment like the black coils of hair, like breath. Oh, precincts of camouflage, of storage, self-command, projection; wisps of self rising like fumes from a spirits glass. The room is flooded up to the ceiling with a standing lake of perception in which we lie like sunken statues flicked by the fins of small impulses. My mind is an underground chamber made of white tiles and rapidly being flooded with rushing blue liquid and rapidly drained. It is part of the waterways of a great city; the Mundus in Rome or the irrigation of the Hanging Gardens. Images float on the liquid.

I count the classical eras of literature and they are like the fruit of a single tree. Around, the orchard of unwritten song, ethnology, birds. For us, the battalions of thoughts welling up at the turns, like knots, of the day; unmetric and uncounted, roughly pooled. All memories become unhooked as the cyclic store, the library of neural rhythms, stored not topologically but by frequency, changes its mensuration. Recoding, they read out. An accelerated film, sprung from the machine language deeps, of cherished events, flickers past on the ceiling. Each 4-bit word becomes 64. All the levels of precision are wrong. The calibration was too coarse. Logic, the positive and negative of the simple squid axon, a single gate, a single volt, the head-on contention of the parties at law, is dissolved in the torrent of spatial relationships. Affect has vanished. All words are false… my thought is moving so fast that it changes in the time it takes to form a word. Words vanish, they are the death of perception, jetsam on the shore of the river, grave goods, the flow stilled or frozen. I can't talk because the words I know have all gone, unusably imprecise, and syntax is the shape of a tree fruitlessly preserved when the technology has moved on to stone. I can't memorize and I can't simulate the Observer. I can't assimilate to my social self.

My breath becomes visible, a dark salamander wisping: disaggregating in violet smoke. Sparks leap from my fingertips.

I press my eye to a crack in the wall and I see a film running there. An ensemble in linen suits, named on the bass drum as the Waltz Mondial

Showband, is playing an Art Deco tango in a palm court. A thin girl in a streamlined dress like Birgitte Helm's is dancing alone to it, on the reflecting floor. She sings in French about the *cabaret du jour et de la nuit* where someone hallucinated in the forest of numbers turns into a hunter chasing a white deer through a real forest which changes into a seventh sea where a white ship is pursuing a lost island which changes into a port where a sailor back from the seventh sea is looking for a Bar Triste which may not even be in that country at all. A girl sings with a smile which is or is not gay. She turns into a snake, then an ermine, then a glass of wine, then a wisp of smoke... I turn away.

What if I took the irreversible step, snapped the anchor-chain, trod the sill? If I vanished into the third level of symbolisation and rush, the beyond where the mind metabolises even itself, in a turbine azure race? What would I see?

8 hours of solid hallucination. Non-figurative! the world of our categories, myths, is a sliver in the progressional masses of Nature. Conches are attributes of Venus, the pink curves speak to a deep store, the berry is nourishment, part of us replaced; but the thousand species of shellfish are neither this nor that; unassimilable; metaphors for experiences no-one has had; and the imperatives are lost in the thousands of lexicon.

I see the levels of air translucent in wisps of heat, ultraviolet, pure flows. I saw the abstract turn to concrete. I saw metaphors split into two halves. Thoughts rise from what is in the stomach and lead back to it. Our habitual rhythms preserve the spaces they once ran through. What if we began producing fundamental metaphors again? what if we let the solo abandon the melody and lead on into the borderless space? what if we destroyed the models?

What then, when the kit of symbolisations, of fictions representing numerical series as plotted lines in cartesian space, energy as fire, mental processes by farming metaphors, thought as words, has collapsed, mutated, each level of symbolization yielding a second level in a rushing triad?

In my bones are a million hollows, tholoi, inscribed paper, where hallucinations play on the white partition. A neural DNA of recombinations, a mouth of new forms. Axioms emerge like snakes on the bottom of a drained lake. The snakes are cold and have dry rough skins, slobbering in mud and rubies. Among the corroded bronze and the silt smoother than silk, the axolotls and the coral in the shape of a man, the premature mechanisations break up into bricks and the bricks wash away into the crumb of the soil. The snake laughs, tongue flickering in a black scroll of theses.

How many distinct shapes can I see at any one moment? I have perhaps nine digits in all, changing their value instant by instant. I can count nine birds… when I look at the tenth, the first two merge. The simple forms are coded to deep ones in store – a million charged laminations each with nine characters. I isolate the changing tip of consciousness itself, the narrow brilliance of focus – and the dark mass of memory sleeping beyond.

Staring at the white wall, I see the universe of perfect tessellation, the hands moving across the vast web of colours and values, an endless codex of ideograms printed on tiles so smooth they fit together without lime; the underlying structure of space.

# CALENDAR RITE

## X1 The Cold River

A brave series of costumes and postures has left me
shivering like someone stripping down to enter a cold river.
A wealth of art and ideas gathered
as adornment, hid physiological facts.
Now there are new eyes
which measure existing assets as void.
What was hidden is the only thing visible.

I cannot take anything with me.
A tea-chest of pen and ink poems, abandoned
a site complex of intellectual positions, powered down
a framework of logical conclusions, rusted out
a soirée of witty remarks, out of date
a shopful of symbolic objects, wiped blank
The pebbles in the river confound their count
only going from one to zero and zero to one.

On the other shore, there will be a whole new terrain.
There is no shape left here, the only heat comes out of my mouth
like a metre that recurs after all the instruments have stopped.
I am cold and the only thing I can burn is my own flesh.
The river is wide and frost-fed
it has a bed of coloured pebbles
which you can grind to make famous pigments.

The need which preceded any signal or adornment
comes into sight, naked and unstable.
It will re-create
what a shift of ground shook into dust.
Maybe my heart will stop in the middle of the river
a gasp of it warmed up for a time with no beat
by a river that doesn't even remember itself
flicking up images on its unmarked surface
reversing out flaws in the eternal present.

## X2 Thematic

What I meant to say was this
The audience surrounded me and
the karaoke machine in the room below was too loud and
the traffic noise coming in through the open window made me
the third biggest sound signal in that air
blocked by superimposition
I can't reach you

It is either one, or nobody,
either here or nowhere

my territory is vanishing and my voice
along with it
stress rattling my ribs as if attenuation of sound
were expression

How small is the space that is inside and authentic
How sweet is the sound
outside the wash from dredging noise
– a jewel for fingertip search

someone was recording the whole thing
capturing a documentary of anxiety
so it can repeat itself.
If I could falsify that record!

## X3 Coloured Dust

On the dish the flowering tree
has three suns blooming on its branches
done in slip, in red blue and black
like paint on an eye,
like a rite to make the solar world change
recorded in calendar pottery.
The void blows into fine forms before falling
back into its ground state
sidling to lose every outline and colour.
The senses make it seem like real fruit.

Find the bottom of the river and curl up as a pebble
it swallows heat and cold and its smoothness is damage
it says what the other stones say
they abrade each other
its colour rubs off as dust and flows towards the mouth.
Patterned stones I collect and arrange
harden out of their native fog of memory in
the grip of my hand. Roll the stones
and scatter them over the boards. Were there peaks?
Did I catch on the pinnacles and clatter off?
did I flow over cobbles and mud?

Pattern dissolving out of the scene
stars on a turning tree
fruit shifting tint delicately from ripe to rotten.
Sun-tree dish shifts colour
where the year grows like fruit
as green, yellow, and red suns
show at the same time.
The suns ripen and turn into flossy white seed-strands
among leaves fading down spills of rare divided tints,
and blossoms that drank now close,
ringing for blank spectra

## X4 Performance Fear

Jump on a bench in the marketplace
*let's do it right here in the car park.*
On a plot of fireweed and broken bricks
you mark off the sacred space and trip through the routine
one more time. From noise pollution to open outcry,
summon up the energies from down in the kidneys.
No props no lights. Either here or nowhere.
The fallen rain washes down a faint glare.

Seize their attention, take
their will away from them, supply
their wish. They don't
seem too happy to pause.
I can't hear my own voice
across the traffic noise and the crowd sounds
just my ribs shaking
with the scale, the thrust, the soar
*What you're afraid of is the most significant thing about you*

a sonorous lapse. a
vain form of light air
which even a ripple would shiver.
You are one of the landless
sharer of the groundless.
Try a gesture of self-love
you could simplify and repeat.
The untouched are incorruptible, you must seek out
the likes of the despised and love them.
A classificatory act
guides you to your cell or enclosed garden
as space breaks up
into a protective system
made of voids

We take the tape back to somewhere quiet
to relive the moment on the edge
all we can hear is layers of noise

## X5 Banal Poem about Falling of Leaves

What lived in a tea-chest now has a filing cabinet
that Luci gave me, kilograms of mouse-nest
and yards of lost speech. It was in 1973
I decided to become a poet, surround myself
with objects I made, verbal objects as it turned out.
Paper recites my stiff words too conveniently
the pages were deciduous and forested.

In 2021 I can see I failed to let it go
it's hard to define why I started out up the hill
and who knows if I got what I came for,
everything is here and it doesn't answer any questions.
What I recall comes up as pictures or dream objects.
What are these coloured pebbles
and what is this river running with?

Stage fright has no voice or shape
it's the lizard brain taking over your senses
the silhouette is of aggression, partly staffed
partly inhuman. It has a voice
no-one admits to, that everybody knows

Maybe everybody at a reading
built the shape I want to see,
the reflexive moment, where the river stands still
complete for a flicker too short for me to read it
before it dispersed from 50 chairs through 50 doorways
into fragments I can't re-link now
into a full tenuity
an enticing emptiness.

I am devising a calendar rite to make things change
with yellow pen on red leaf-web
with red sap on yellow cotton tissue
to inscribe a decaying message on a decaying medium
the colours of the leaves must change again
and allow a new arrangement

## X6 Performance High 1

Voluble and mercurial
I stare out at the rows of chairs,
unsteadily heaving the air I will separate into sound
running on steps at varying height.

The silence finally invites me to declaim.
I cycle through a reaction away from social realism
and head-on confrontation of the power elite
to showing a fine object as limited-stimulus field,
at its edge is the line between being and not-being.
The alien cultures appear, to rehearse
how a mind imitates the time that runs past it,
reciting what is always being staged.
It responds to beauty, integrity, and complexity;
the abandonment of durable arguments
acts as a relief from daily oppression.

I reach a still point, calmed by sea and sun, but
a string is not altogether in tune,
they had something else in mind.
In fine, they are on the outside
of this magnificent inside,
the flight is tangled in the trees, quite high,
rather somnolent.
The lifted sound dissipates through flesh
which is dense and juicily moisture-rich
a battery of baffles set in rows, indeed.
Bagged and drowned, it loses kinetic energy
so as to surrender information
which was heading out towards the open air
quite creamy and distributed in
beautiful sine waves
symmetrical and self-repeating.

# X7 Performance High 2: *A Romance of the Docks*

I spread my hand in the gesture of "one bestowing a wish"
and signal everyone to shut up.
Tonight's theme is to cut out autobiography and go
straight to patterned collective myth,
the imaginary in geometry.

Such a return of buried archaic worlds to light
would have to pick its way past the beautiful tableaux of myths
staged and lit by the courtiers of national ego –
needles that sew dust into a narrative and its hero.
My *Romance of the docks* is an afternoon lost in the world
of mid-century propaganda,
alluring stories of a leisure class in ideal clothes.

Photographs open onto a beckoning space,
a glittering demon world which, as we say yes to it,
engulfs us in its generosity and authenticity.
How would we reconstruct the past
once we discard these traps of the invisible with their discreet deities?
Suppressing the murmurs of the un-narrated
and converting code-breaking revolt into mimicry
it is the false as a decorative couture of the true.

By the sea-shore, we follow another geometry,
the small rock clutching a blast of air-holes
recites the vortex of open seas,
the Western Seaways as the circles along which a culture spread
Celtic and insular, centreless and pervasive,
a chamber scooped by echoes and filled with exchanges
following the circuits of the ocean.
It answers the question, what is social structure
with the preparation of a series of symbolic objects
holding the imaginary within a silent hand.

In the excitement I start to compose the next one.
Hearing the inaudible, no, sous-entendu, no, collusive, no, implicit
and vanquishing the invisible, no, imperceptible, no, hegemonic,
and dredging images from underwater, no, kept in the dark, no,
interred, no, invested, crushed, no, suppressed, to
walk upon the surface of a new earth.
Phallocratic, no, bureaucratic, no, paratactic
surges into the realms of my worn out, no, drugged, no,
languid and loose, no lush, sensibility.
I watch the shared scenes descend on the rows of chairs,
it holds for a fraction of a second
and exits at the window. Their shared stake is their own
and they rebuild it, crushing what I say.
The poet moves among the people
like a fish through soup

## X8 Gnosis

Heresy
is a sound from underneath the river

the Sibyls gleam quite naked white among the white birch trees
the birches are the women and they are green when stripped
they act without memory finding trails of heat
singing words I don't understand
*eat of my flesh – and swallow your reason*
*I look at the screen and don't see the picture that you do*
*I don't show up in your photograph*
*the poem is a paper priest, a dead guardian*
the red smear of the fungus drips on the birch flank
the green sap of the birch wells from the cut
*the state is a wraith breathing out falsehoods*
*the archives go from bluster to blocking out*
the mushroom is a biochemical lens
nourished by your heart and flesh
through which a whole new world pours
the mushroom grows back through the eye and feeds on its light

the Sibyl of the waste ground speaks,
Veleda of the nest in the squat clarifies
they emerge from the pool in green sunlight, to tell me
*the life that fills you is not theirs*
*and is the knowledge they don't have*
*they wipe out what you know to form an institution*
*the frozen senses are flooding you with false memories*

those drops from a film of blurred light
through which the damage of the real world is replenished,
shake, and the buildings shake with them
the image peels off the eye which
walks off as insect
scuttling at bottom of green scummed pools
where gold grows in tendrils and fronds

ink flows off paper effacing
blackletter fits of rage,
title deeds setting the munificence of egoism out

*I read their chronicles and a second meaning*
*stands out clearly, as*
*in the folios black and white reverse themselves*
*memory is a trap for the beguiled*
*property is the drug of the powerful*

## X9 Carrion Crows

Suspended
from the Gothic projections near the ceiling
curling out of the air strung with sound
protected
by mercery of state and post-mortal chill
sanctity reflected in counter-gifts
heat chilled before it can spread.
In patristic prissiness
and auratic hauteur
the carrion judges intertwined and vested
are bishops citing themselves as provenance
in chains of authorities passing skin products on down
to apostolic heirs in sleets of dudgeon,
inaugurators of verdict and vindict,
keepers of categories of inaudible people.
The judges are exotic birds, beautifully plumed
as they eat human flesh and hawk it up again
for their young and their acolytes.
The judges are fabulous birds of loathing
grinding the calories out of stopped organs
they smell out guilt and scrape for the evidence of penance.
Fear is the music it all moves to.
They wear flounced robes of office and anoint
themselves with oils pressed from Socotran trees,
the acolytes wear short skirts and tennis shorts,
they are eager and pliable. They repeat everything
in chorus and at deafening volume.
Too young to have faces, in whiteness of candidacy,
sedulous aspiration masked by thin irony.

Pinned and flaked under
the millimetrical scrutiny of approval
how much I admire the complexity of your reasons
for disliking my work, and how I am hushed by your malign monologue.
"His organ of speech is too big

and his toes don't match.
It's authentic 1978
but provincial and low-end 1978.
The apical space slips on
its beautiful attenuation
by cutting people out,
those thick in tongue and coarse in appetites.
Refining discrete domain into true sophistication
needs the debitage of certain graded people.
We call it structured strata-building.
Even our garbage is finely divided.
His assets are not fine enough to be worth appraising,
or curated with our precious objects;
although a part of a recognised regional stratum of low culture
the obscurity of the time segment in which he inhaled, and froze up,
deprives it of piquancy."

"The solidity of the emotional dish on offer
is non-virtual in a peasant-like way
and makes the level of ideas inaudible.
The frank acquisition of symbolic objects –
like someone buying a car, for God's sake –
is low, where asceticism and self-withholding are higher.
That obsession with barbarians is firmly crude rather than naïve."

## X10 A Route March in the Cultural Field

The *agon* is a suit to acquire status, it
bestows the right to speak.
Chance is the origin of space
that is, the lot in the air before it falls.
The square of the vanquished is pinned out as negative territory.
The players are profane but the rules are sacred,
this is a game that must be lost.
The field, staked out till the last one returns; the course,
*Agon* and claim for honours; the judges
make rulings for recording in orthogonal incisions.
The tally of the runners makes
a reference set of four hundred
selectively admitted, in direct rivalry.
The phase of differentiation
disperses what was originally complete.

In deep water, helms set the keels
towards haven and the celebration wharves.
*Agon* is a means of knowledge, the delicate scale
where centimeters of extent recite
the strengths of an organ. The thickness of inner waters.
The shore captures the deviant anatomies of the deep,
the wreck zone is echeloned
above the beach, palings mark how far a ship is driven
into its fear space.
What is known of you except by rivals,
do you even catch sight of it, without spite or malice?

White-coated guardians award the points, mark them up,
and superimpose the test subjects
on a "tally board" we all read together.
Packed in shared reactions, the interchangeable
shift position. Differentiation as damage,
scavenger garage. Strain draws
new organs from the wreckage of old ones.

Hazards cleared
from the fairway,
raising of the rough into the stylised;
where features intersect and bind you call it a self.
Dissimilating into an empty quadrant
what goes further recedes and diminishes;
for, *whose terrain is this?*
still waits for any answer.
How many were better than you and in what ways,
who were you similar to?

A magic double hanging your actions from its masts,
the bronze boats sunk in the gravel at Nors, safe haven under ground,
are controllers of real ships in fatal forerunning.
Earth jewel beaten fine, twelve centimeters long, to scale,
bronze strakes wrapped in gold leaf hull
fit for no earthly water.
*Spinkel og dobbelspidse* slender and double-prowed craft
strake-grasped and unripplefast
to sail beneath the earth and track the night sun
to gleam like ash, float like stones.
The judges work malice on the ships: to sink them
or let them swim. Gold foil hull is weak ego.

When someone calls out your name and sinks the toy boat
your lot is falling to a ground.
The rivals are pulsing the little vessel with their feet
tearing and crushing
smearing gold leaf in mud
in frenzy to destroy
till there's nothing left.
Your voyage is over, the leftovers
eaten by crabs.

## XII The Cologne Mani Codex

If I open my hand you can see this object hidden in it.
It is Mani's autobiography.
The writing is of the fifth century
and it is the size of a matchbox
to be read by a lens, and hidden again.
Written behind glass in lettering a millimetre high, signalling
the essentials of the cosmos, in a religion of light
trapped in dead and corrupt matter.
It is as small as its handwriting, as large
as the stage of noon.
The convex jug exposes
the fall of solar splendour
in the mystery of captive light.

People heard the truth and wrote it down,
hidden from whatever had eyes,
the glare of malice
finds it out and destroys it.
On one of the tiny vellum squares
a line has a few words in the Greek of the time.

The millimetrical scale is where the world is intact
and light is even finer,
thin enough to exit from
a whole world of ashes, enactments and toxins.

From a remote place of burial
of the fatal and forbidden scripture,
a voice is audible from leaves stuck together.
The last fifty leaves are unreadable, or yield
single characters in a plain of waste,
of features lost
where the marriage of light and darkness fell,
our guide is taken away from us in the trackless.
Sink to find a fallen star –

the path that would draw us back to the heart of the light,
a return to the undamaged as colours fall away
beaten thin across a spectrum and a sky.

## X12 Non counterpart

there would be a counterpart poem about a body
and its entanglement
but I showed her the poem circa 1994
and she couldn't see what any of it meant
so the counterpart reaction didn't exist
and the poem vanished in the wake ripple

If you can't be both loved and understood
it is better to be a counterpart of a living person
while signs flock and wheel quite without meaning
wing pairs flying off in two different directions

I can't get across to you
you are the inside of my outside
you think what I mean can be more logically defined
and will then disappear
put that sharpened knitting needle away

it was something about abstraction and the acquisition of tools and assets
what was made of emptiness and fills with everything

## X13 Inside and Out

The skin that distends to let assets in
shrinks to let them slip out again
the whole heat slides out of my mouth
the light drains out of the hole and faces up at the sky.

The reds evanesce and the blues thin down and fade
the sound signal inverts and the light draws down
the objects turn to air
the petals turn to grey
the grey seeps down to a dot, a haze.

So much effort
to externalise inner objects
whose value may stabilise at zero
the verbal tracks look like the primary objects
reaching the edges of the project

chilling agitation
through manic exercise of racked faculties
to build an inner calm.

In the palazzo hewed from hard lime
the carving of Diana shows the subtle influence of a tidal goddess
where the outside of the world
is the inside of the body.
Olive trees sip on limestone hills,
the limestone creatures swim in the sea
to the melody of conches.
Tiny floating specks of moonlight
mimic the action of the moon
lapping back and forth with the waves
before going down to make chalk.
Narrative sinusoid delay line,
exchanging of inside and out;
the coiled waterways and their refined symmetries

are ebbing through mirrored recesses.
The hollows of the elaborated void and their underwater spirals
are scored on parallel tracks.
The tyrants of the mercantile towns
eject their rich hours onto the visual fixation,
the grandiose recording of self and its court,
so inside becomes palazzo and outside becomes status objects
connected through fine pipes and quills
floating back and sounding
drifting in and out on the tide.

Here among the half-outer objects in pure oral light
there is no inside and out.
Lapping back and forth with the waves
I am trying to make chalk;
the wrapping of fingers
that flung itself around a hard form
and woke its nerves in contact only
reached a strict edge where knowledge runs out.
The objects fill the poems which turn into objects
so I become larger with the ones I acquire
and they become larger as they come close
and as the pattern locates its parts and comes to a head
I am emptying again.
Why do you like these patterns,
and, why do you think they are yours?
why don't you like all the patterns?

# X14 Dissident

We are going there together and so
I do what you want?
I should say the same things as you
because you own them?
this I, body and mind,
I am a distortion of you?
So teach me
the line of the investments and the entwined and the enrobed
what has eaten into memory
and sunk through into unconsciousness
the damp that permeates the planking
a statistical smoothing of
a thousand repetitions of
a didactic line.
No, I prefer what I don't know and is just out of reach.
I can show
you what slipped through my grasp.

The dust sparkling in the void teaches me my course
at the end of the third year I was nowhere
at the end of the fifth we had precocious hopes of me
in the tenth year I had seized the pattern
of what is blank and areally covering
and I found no one to applaud my results
and in year 40 I had memorised the void
which had moved rotating calendrically
as a flat film on a turning cylinder
curved to falsify memory

I make your mirror rot. A dissident
struck from the rolls, waiting outside the doors
in the quiet of the abandoned yard
the cool of the ruins
free in the large dissolved structures.

You have an algorithm to flatten the peaks,
to step up the troughs, to erase my face.
Signal? jamming? damaged substrate,
exquisite desensitisation
a mirror in which I cannot see myself.
Being non-corporate is disaffection, or is
the pristine, unmediated,
carnal and local, of the terroir;
the fault where new information wells up
and is off message.

A national epic bleeds from the cuts
kinetic damage at both sides of the edit
a surf of white noise rolling from the suppression.
We were flaws in a false music
that has been ragged and sated
ripped and sifted from its cadence
by its sediment of sweetness.

# A Cold River 2

Sibyls stand in the river and speak to me
they say, I cannot cross
there is no other bank

The flashes leave the valley as their gift
drowning in new suns
in a pool of the river the wrack grasps at its limbs
and loses its substance

Pattern is sharp because the soft parts have rotted
it lingers as a slower motion slackens its grip
to catch the senses and draw down what is detained
to emerge in the decay of light
coloured dust in wreaths over a void

They say, your words are static and the river falsifies them
they make a smoke that tries to return
to the wood and straw possessions of the fire
the plume of your heat travelling through the river's body
is one gasp in a thousand closed lips of chill

Differentiation splits many symmetries and is reversible
you emerge from the ice fitted with features which the river forgets
heresy is a set of stone walls that dissolve into quadrilateral smoke
knowledge of the unpredictable is Sibylline wealth

Poems and prophesies share in falls of metre
yours soaked in past time, and ours in the river that has no shore –
headless prosodies without a self
from roll of beats to head of motif

Floodwater as it ebbs leaves a skin of fruitful dirt
delicacy of silt softens coarse debris
staves dabbed with paint will flower where they fall
crack willows will fall, but stricken, strike root on the far bank

ash which flows will clear a cold fairway
world will slip out of your models and your hand will curl around a toy
you will let your words flow
under the river and its streams

## AA: Calendar Rite

The rite lasts for twelve days of Chaos
interstitial, while twelve serial months of order build

high water unfastens the plane of sight
there is a shade before colour
a speck before dust – a pallor before shape
a twilight before the stars – land under rain
the sky with every object waiting to be painted
rotates from light towards quenching
where snow turns to limestone
milk to ash – p to zero
birch to willow – feathers to snow

a flat scene winds on a curving surface
you turn the cylinder and the picture moves away from you
the colour comes off the sky
as the roller turns backwards
turning into flakes too light to fall
a decaying scene blows off a decaying medium
the dust runs out to the edge and catches all the rain
it swallows the light and the space swallows it
slowly spinning in the absence of air

a static world is replaced by a static art
each part completing another
Time trapped in waves that never break and
a dawn that never shines
hiding the rim of an unmoving sun
beautiful pale figures without pulse
conservative return to the loved event
traps repetition with declining affect

the Year Child is young and very bored
she wants everything
starting with language and sight

she demands a whole world for her toy
and new gifts every day
we explain that she has to draw them first
all she has to do is catch the things she is unhappy without
she draws lands and seas on a flat piece of fabric

the child refuses to draw difficult things
those countries never emerge
I can remember what they were called
but not what they look like
she is impatient and wants to see new things

the Year Child starts to grow very fast
the queen of a badly drawn country
lays down deep stores of sleep
we insist that clothes are made of textiles
and houses of ceramics. The king of Bessarabia
sets his crown on the ground
he cuts letters of beech and letters of birch
he hoops casks of each and eats feasts of both
he plants the staves in a row
and catches sounds in the trees

the December storms blow down trees and buildings
a thousand fiddles hanging up
distract the gale
into hearing its own voice
channelled through apertures and softened by baffles
until its chaotic force becomes slender
and the separate sound refines
the unfinished bodies of calendar monsters

in the river, warm layers float up
the ice on its surface melts

**AXIS OF SYMMETRY          CALENDS          YEAR-NEWEL**

## Y14 Poem of gofyn and diolch, being of request and thanks for a gift

The proposal is that I should praise your feats and facts
extol the stability of your graphite cores
and the cellular niches of your tenements

while ornately perpetuating
the sensitivity of the rich
the refinement of their hedonism
matching the differentiation of goods

In the corporate video
I will recite the villainy of the defeated
their prizing of sodomy, heresy, and bastardy
their defective grasp of their inferior status

I will attribute the apex of language to the social apex
rarity of form stalking up to high prices
exclusivity as in a Bond Street shop
the aura of speech lit by an elite presence
like armour shining around an aristocratic frame
as if glowing from transmuted flesh.
If it carries only a few feet, before sullying,
my role is to record and distribute it,
in language cascading around the body like clothes

I looked for myself
in the reflective wall circling the haven city
The principal line of division
attempts to capture the symmetry of light and darkness
in flat sheets or rigid frames,
and I found only a cell where
the substrate was scraped bare
that wall which jerks like a pupil and shines like one

In the enchanted legend for the manager
the great pipes run snug along the edge
of what is visible and what isn't
returning time in flux to where things were.

He embraces and circles a glass bowl
and finds sediment swirls as alluvium,
scrabbles through mud and gravel
He arranges the partitions of an uncleared land.

A scene is framed by a cooling crystal
organised by liquids in close rooms.
The colour of the cladding
is serene and detains the gaze.

If I magnify the mighty, in return
I make an invoice and request
for a splendid home and its grounds

My invoice specifies
the star-shaped Anatolian ceramic
of unknown purpose but with Bektaşi associations
prying open the edge of a secret world

the Cycladic figurine with its paint intact
the Ralph Toft slipware jug from the seventeenth century
cream-coloured slip on an orange body,
naive image of an expensively dressed man
the Norwegian tapestry with the Biblical narratives.

You fund my production
the skeins wrapping scenes and titles together,
claims set out in pictures of founding acts.
The tracing of a city plan and the acceptance of heritage.
The binding of the fathers, the capture of the ancestral mounds.
Monuments on the skyline. And the narrative unrolling as title deeds.
Directing the past as the roadway on which property rights arrived.

Let me present an account for personal services.
In return for malice and dissidence,
a wealth of cold and darkness
a cry of rotating repetition
hanging for an acknowledgment
wheeling words door to door on a barrow
lacking that food which the living eat

## Y13: Outside and In

In a grave, the assemblage might keep the shape of a body, because its parts were adornments, clinging to a person in the site of the ego. The interment is the size to let a human through, a concealed door, for passage. A search is started because the carrier has to be complete before it can lift the ego into a new state. So one might be writing a book in the image of a body made of charged objects. They carry such varied forms of damage. A thousand wrong orders, resolved in a perfect symbolic machine. At the end of the gathering one might stand up and start the journey.

Lost reference. Saw once but could not find again. Star-ray ceramic associated with Bektaşi Order but of unknown use. While searching for pictures of fake Neolithic figurines.
Was seen by collector but he could not buy it. His memory may be at fault. Blue and gold? Maybe a fake, a bazaar antiquity, made up for the Chelsea market.
Had a contractor knock up a mock-up.
Cannot remember if it was ceramic or bronze. Or if I saw it at all.

A proposal that a poem is first an arrangement of objects, and then an operation on them and then a verbal object which follows the phases of the operation. The project for creating a storehouse for these outputs. It is like a gift shop.

A terret ring in coloured enamel and a La Tène motif, shining like an eye. And a fragment of fossil narcissism, owner's pride carried by his horse, which becomes the *epitheton ornans* for his prowess. Adorement, adornment. Freezing on contact with cold reality, tucked into a sheltering layer of earth.

The light buried inside the body traces the self through its intimate distortion zone, chemically enhanced and corroded on the way to its new exit. The light trap subjects the chalk hillside to duplication, reversals, partial repeats, distortions, violations of symmetry. As its energy decays its contents migrate, floating on waterways that loop and shoal. It scatters around the sky in the shape of a world.

dig to find a buried star
rays of ceramic earth fused into surpassing hardness
aggregating metals to itself
shining from deep darkness
ancient silicates fused into glass
concentric rings of defensive mirror panel

The ceramic is part of an operation I cannot see. We hear a verbal overlay in a language I do not know. The words are slow, and may be a telestic spell or the spiel of a dealer in the bedesten. It is now a star with twelve rays, with separation from the body. It is a starfish and has a surface like a brass coffee-jug, for taking direct heat. Its limbs are set in the same plane, at rest from their function. It has come a long distance but cannot move. It is like a section through a celestial star, radiating in two dimensions only.

*Ich-Gestein*, the I-mineral, bands of self
overloads eased by chemical exchange
growing slowly and settling solidly in pure lodes
the banks of melancholy the stalls of alabaster
the bursts of metabolic excess displace the earth
silting up in a wealth captured by lethargy

Bodiless and glutted
a patron who costs the earth who sells the earth
who creates the earth who spins the earth
who dowses the earth in blackness who buries the light in a wet field
who stops and starts time
who tapers the telescopes who accelerates their rifling
who freezes the pulse who clears the channels
whose appetite is consonant with the real, whose deficit is adequate to
                                              [what is coming
whose rhythm strophes the inexistent
who dyes the chalk white
who turns the seasons, who divides the dialectic

The *fondo d'oro*, a scrap of gold leaf clasped inside two sheets of glass, like a piece of light that has failed to make its way out again. A gold tear, closed on itself, fragile as a human feeling. However thin, the gold is never transparent.

the optic appliance reports a real land
which is hammered and drawn, sheared and stained,
heightened and partly deleted, raised and multiplied
set down in strange shapes
shimmering with rhetoric
held up by phantoms
ruined by symbolism, perfected by sentiment

subjects the limestone caves
to inversion and reconnection
a space scooped out
by a sound reverberating

Birds' claws were interred with a body in a Bronze Age howe. Twelve large ones and four small. The narrative records the glass fells which cannot be climbed without a device that has no care for gravity or the thinness of air. Which walks on glare as if on dry sand or a causeway. The traveller needs a map and the skills of birds. The glass fells are a mistranslation for mountains of light, a word like *glare* existing before they ever saw glass.
The stretching of memory, thin tissue
opened by a new air, like an eye
lighter than glare
a wing covered with nerves
shakes out, tearing off bits of sheath
a verse of words kept as a new organ
directing the body in entire and ornate patterns
*Catch me if I fall.*

## Y12 Gnarls and Snibs

The origin of style
in a fault of the senses
or, back to the substrate
a cry
enacting the state of fine organs
details of the throat
expanded into information over a waste of air
physiology attenuated becomes an abstraction
by the spacing of air molecules

"What does this authenticity mean
except the slighting
of civil authority?
What is this aesthetic energy
but a loss of proportion?
This claim to do what he likes
gives a prior place to impulses
which are no more than body parts
scaled up, lit, and put on display.
Who authorised your feelings?

These are menial and non-château impulses
series of misshapen small bones in finicky arrays
like a root that could not find the nutrients
and scrawled and strained and went off axis
like a snail whose spiral has slid off its route.
A superimposed grid detects
snibs and gnarls. Impulses, intuitions, asymmetry –
these we wring the neck of.
We are looking for someone
whose feelings are superior,
smoothed and flowed like ceramics,
the porcelain sensations
of the proper and *précieux,*
those who put the prissy into prestige."

It was as clear as a fail in an ideological test, I
am a centre of insolence,
a ragwort on your lawn.
The sequel after 40 years, a trail
of failures, exclusions, shut-outs, lost manuscripts,
a voice in the cellar of the theatre
and a style growing out into the empty sector
warming the frozen river

## Y11 The Origin of Space

the millimeters separate truth from silence
they slide towards a slit where they escape
wholly, behind the origin of light
the sound is sucked back into tiny flaws in the wood
it shrinks down to grains like sand
and does not shed its charge
sustained by the periods of the same metre

the sound returns first and what follows it is
a slit in the air that raw space falls out of
heavy like burnt river pebbles
splintering like wrenched bone
sliding like a shovelful of embers

this is the birth of abstraction
the mouth uttering a hidden world
a frame setting where the void loses its memory
near a gash that tries to swallow and crush space

the magniloquent stone and glass make heresy stand up
express symbols in a figurative cycle
They take living space and transform it.
Where we are together.
is the place where inside and out match up
and you become weightless, rising from the ground.
It is made of stone that dissolves
and alters the air as abstract ideas
its outline is the counter-perimeter of critique
the interior castle

## Y10 The Catalogue of Ships

The *Golden Vanity*. The *Psychedelic Dreadnought*. The *Drain Treader*. The *Virtualised Hull*. The *Chelsea Ferry*. The *Scrap Montage*. The *Landfall the Unknown*. The *Smiling Medusa*. The *Glass Tower*. The *Elizium Shore*. The *Pond Life Beaker*. The *Pigfish*. The *Serenely Incoherent*.
Cadaver ships, fragmented at the jetsam line
Wrecked when the stress-test grasped the facts.

In the red zone, where anatomy, rivalry, and
style pour out of the same pipe
where a surface tells the history of its becoming
where strain and rips tell the drag of the invisible and strange;
pitting of the shared objects.
Sifting of the shared debris
a telltale of deep structures
where grams of surface erosion
attract the judges for hours of huddling
a hash of cross-hatching on the marking sheets.

The hulls dissolve in pilot error.
One numbed by his own stupefied energy
one flying like a bird
one dissimilating into empty territory, number one
in the wilderness, tyrannical and emaciated.
One dissolute in pale mimicry.

Action during loss of consciousness can nonetheless
be observed by others
an apex raised on foreign assets
can be defended by deflected envy

The fleet of wood is damaged by sailing
riddled with voids by shipworm
its boards eaten by coloured waters.
The vexed frames turning eventually to bone
secure the bed of the fairway,
scoured with whorls and pits, erosion holes for pins

continuing the spirals of water.
An anthology subdued by the market
is the zone to separate contenders.
Losing your way before landfall,
a cell defined by serial numbers locates an agonist
at their extreme point where awareness gives out.
Fallen on the field where the game was lost,
losing impetus,
fatigue traces a self, quite pure, spoor, cell, shell,
unable to move any further, ejecting the hard anatomy
of a new radiation that
wrenches loose-set vertebrae apart to bend a new lift of wings,
alien and transcendent, raised on arcs breaking up the flat land,
on an axis uninflected and fledged with pure velocity.

Pennants flutter to track
The *Ice Passage Finder*. The *Stripy Sides*. The *Deep Calm Beneath the Waves*.
The *Towey Coracle*. The *Star Swept*. The *Spray-on Authenticity*. The *Flat Pack and Fold-Up*.
The *Celery Raft*. The *Oak and Brass*. The *Reflection of Asymmetry*.

## Y9 Carrion Crows Stay Up Late

This is your chance to open the doors for me,
to let my sound into a big clear space.
I have some modest statement prepared –
Big space? not very big space? a negative amount?
I'm being athetised by the thrice holy? Run out by the role enforcers?
Distorted by orthodoxy? Execrated by the sacrosanct?
A speck that inspection picks away at?
Deterior by the criteria?
Out of hearing of the orient stars?
An obloquy to the impositions,
Forsaken by the superstructure?
The earth will cover over my mouth?
They hang near the ceiling
releasing corrosive and finely tapered
benignity as thin, as fastidious, as a skewer.
"Movements are drawn from a repertoire
every thesis is surrounded by a nebula of versions
but this is our realm of verdict
and we exercise our freedom
to preclude that of others
in solidarity, transcendence. Light follows our fingers in the air,
nimbus fits to our heads like curls.
In a voluptuous game we play
our wish moves from rule to law
setting a stable value, the elevation
on a mound of degradation. Ascent to the skyline
where we control silence."

"There is no creation of value here
no aperture into prestige alliances
selective long-distance high value gift exchanges.
The slight substance of preciosity
is not at his tongue's tip.

To have read the wrong books
to know the wrong people
is ultimately to float odd gestures, unfit for the precincts.

Let his records be deleted! Raise the site value by erasing him!
Let him sleep in the yard!"

Possessed by some voluble and not very urbane demon
I am swept up with a broom and locked out
I clutch my papers
and fill my pockets, state my claim outside the court
I make a sound swallowed by space folding up small.
Use wands to stake out a stage in the yard, in the dark. Freedom and
                                                                [plenitude
for as many as will.

## Y8 In a River

a raft of dead crows floats downstream
their strakes have turned to bronze
and their feathers to gold
rotting gold trickles off in a blackened wake
losing signal in the cleansing water
their sockets have eyes of quartz
for them to trap false knowledge in

the river is
filled with hidden objects
half-outer half-inner
half burnt half drowned
half words half sense data
shoals and sunken trees
snagging the fairway in a thousand parts
birches for snow, the river's
trees are green willows, cracked and toppled
from shore to shore, with voices of Sibyls, saying
*space is blasting out of our bodies*
*stones of heresy wrought in gnosis*
*like a shell forming over the invisible*
*series of projective architecture*
*urban plazas and fairways*
*networks of materials*
*the passive and extensive captured by symbolism*
*gives an outside for such an interior*

*acephalous and with many voices*
*a cry at the origin of storms*
*we flow through your texts like floodwater*
*the light is within us, the moon and stars move*
*to recite our impulse*
*follow a cycle of*
*the serene and the burning up*

## Y7 Performance High 3: Sparse Terrestrial Rim

That touch of mania
like a small glass of sambuco
archaic and intact, like a separate throat
speaking in several voices at rapid tempo
build a square to release it safely
look, you can set fire to the fumes draft.
Cold river unclenched, flaring off in high streams;
Cold heart stretching its beat, warming every limb.
Piety towards the accelerating chaos,
stack the dials pointing towards danger
sirens wailing the sky into their open gullet
tissue choking with rich fluids.

A fear unfolding dizziness and chills
locking the knees
and burying the voice down in the pit
of flight reaction.
The tightening of the vessels
and loss of soul to the darkest hollow
to the waving treetops
I move towards the source of anxiety
I face front and signal for everyone else to fall silent.

The poem consists of a ring of metaphors
each one repeating the other
blazing a kind of exit path
through which we escape. Through skin cells
the dependence on arriving radiance binds the physiology of the viper,
and its metabolic shutdown for nine months a year
mimics the action of the celestial bodies,
substances from outside breaching the sparse terrestrial rim.
The metaphors allege
the social order is a captivity or winter;
the poem defends Memory, which as the light of stars
swallows darkness, drifts through night and interment.

Signals pierce the sky rim in either direction, it is
an eye smeared with dust
pulsing open to an unknown emitter,
the subsoil is littered with dream objects,
the poem wakes under alien stars.

The weight escapes us and I am lifted
on waves of pure light.
The poems fly past the rows of seats
touching no-one. In profound tranquillity, they apply
their energy to digestion.
It was the *lineation* that went wrong.

## Y6 Performance High 4: Altyn-Dagh

The room is a boat where we float together,
where we breathe to make headway, the poem reports that
This is the geography, this is the gradient.
There is a mountain from which you can descend any way
to one side you become European
to one side you become Chinese
down one slope you become Siberian and drive reindeer
down the next you become Central Asian and grow apricots.
Before the coloured dust traps the senses
with their mortally repeating patterns
before the self sinks into a body,
at the apex you can hear all languages
and see light before it is divided:
lucid sheets of snow and gold.
You can ascend in forfeit of experience, defeaturing
to become wraiths floating in shining pairs,
singing tunes for the acquisition of a body.

Lifted on the roar in my ears
I saw the screen of language, the soft lattice
taking shape as a thing like a law
as a score like orchestral music
as a swarm made out of human beings
in imitative tiny gestures following the line of impulses
at a delay, with error. With exaggeration
of my subtle moues and nuances – how basic!
A melodrama with pure vice and pristine virtue, heavy-footed
and I say
suppose we all behaved in an ideal way, detecting each other's feelings
lifted up by ideals, holding nothing back,
respecting the weak and defying the strong
– preferring theories to food. Could you sustain this
for 45 minutes without a rest?
It weakens as they flex and lounge,
like – like Elvis on barbiturates. What is this – *they* control it and not *me*?

Moving these humans around is no easier than reframing
the shuttered concrete of this lecture hall
into a taller shape.

In the excitement I start to compose the next one,
aspire to being suave, to being Prussian,
to be refined, no, attenuated, no, subtle, scant. Wispy.
To hold the perfected social state to their heads, no,
at their feet, no, in their clutches, under their noses.
To erase our alienation, to radiate their wretchedness,
to make a loan against our loss, to make a bid
on our dilapidations, set a mission statement
for the ruins management.
To straighten the coastline. To make the slums vertical.
To redress iniquity. Bring the errors of perspective
closer. Bridge the jetstream.
To caress intimate areas. To share out symbolism.
Strain empathy to the max. Bring the distantiation home.
Drape the windows with the horizon.

To voice self esteem, no, identity, no, amour-propre.
Do I mean to unroll a role, to carry out a doubt.
To fade into a figure of speech?
To capture some social rule or another?
To leap upon a trestle and defend the finest
hesitations?
Cast my image into a glass tower? Collapse in an art deco bar?

Are they still here? these Trotskyites and 5th Monarchy men?
I fragment as they disperse.
That live space is the screen for light of unknown origin
jumping and scattering between us and outside us
which reacts to all our movements, in an unsteady expanse
rushing to devour its own perimeter.
It ejects flickers bearing its shape,
thin and gleaming. we crop them in armfuls
The images froth up, spill over. Mop up.

## Y5 Jealousy

*axe shearing vertebrae*
*feathers mottling with the oxygen of blood*
*a gizzard for the cat*
*light bones opening up*
*a fluttering above the ground*

*the simply superior*
*which knocks me back*
*that huge fluency and concision*
*dramatic without preplanning*
*its love of human beings*
*giving the soul its fill*
*the feeling of abundance*
*decades do not erode*
*this bond under which*
*I fall silent*

*a stripping of protection*
*that loses all measures*
*as the sound without flaws*
*pours in it's perfect*
*because I am picking up*
*that feeling of flow*
*of objects flying through the air!*

*the skin wraps round the world*
*and where they touch there is a sound*
*the skin says, this is my soul*
*it has seized me*
*so that the flesh is all eyes*
*faithful, shifting*
*shape in the intermittent light*
*the soul says, I am trapped, the music*
*is me wrenching at the stitches*

## Y4 The North Circular Motorway at Silver Street

the sound of the lorries and cars was like an ocean
and the voices cancelled each other out
it was a smooth even roar of hiss
and null energy made my skull shake
the words in my head broke up before features emerged
the high-rises had many cells
and the concrete felt like a wave of dulling sound
I could not make out which face was me
nor which thoughts were mine
I could not see my home
I was like an exact ear
that picked up every sound and held it steady
but sense came there none
where the peaks met the troughs
and the end faded into the beginning

you want it artsier, you want you to be more like you
my head is like a drain which sound clears through
I can hear every syllable
but the language is no longer human

a bank of fumes and fly-dust pretending to be air
white noise devours and speeds up all energies
clear signal is what it breaks down
there is a voice inside
or there will be
or there was
what film is this the score to?

we are all hearing the same thing, it is saying
we can't hear each other

## Y3 Theme with Loss of Variation

This blast of fetid air calls itself a city
this pebble bank of damaged signs
inscribes you in a cell.
Spat out by space to hiss a charge of air
this is what I meant to say.

I want to refine the tune and confine its reach
I am surfing on hostility, turning on
circuits that use noise to step up the signal
sipping energy out of abuse.
A pattern reproducing itself
a distortion of the waste field
a true and fitful melody

I try to separate signal from noise
melody decays into something else
to flatten the curve and expand its reach

you can't put the music back into the karaoke machine
and if I was a car I'd be a lot louder
and I could actually hear my own thoughts

infiltrated through a millimetre gap from outside
past noise reducers and force multipliers
under the brass music
vain territory bearing sound
from a wider reach of silence

If my feelings were louder
they would crush other feelings like a karaoke beat
if my feelings were smaller
they would get sucked straight into the air conditioning inlet.
What they dislike most about you
is the single most precious and authentic thing.
It feels like a good time to swap that one!

My head sank into the noise like rushing water
my body turned blue up to my neck
when I was partway across the river
the rotting logs burst into bud
when I was halfway over the river
the heat lashing from my eye
frayed great holes in the living water
I hauled deep gasps of cold and hacked it small
I struck to the heart and lungs of the river and seared them
five plumes of steam stood up from my fingers
my legs snagged on the riverbed high and dry

Light has found an exit, there is
an inside with no outside
a momentary distortion of the air

the outcome of attriting territorial struggle
is a niche on the millimetre scale
a flash in the nick of spectrum
asking for mutated and miniature organs
*that's too small to be a self*

## Y2 Coloured Dust 2

This is the reverse of burning
where cold dissolves shapes to a pristine crystal blank
every object waiting to be painted
with its knowable marks and colours
before words, all substances are equal
edgeless

What was manic repletes itself, acquires dominance,
fixes patterns above the flux,
becomes satiated, seeps out through invisible cracks, finds
that everything that has been alive will rot down.
As the eye stabilises
it sees everything moving away
losing the colours by which their truth was knowable
deteriorating in a still frame.
There is a lethargy of forms. The wave cycles towards dissipation,
the symbolic machine loses energy in repetition,
the game cannot quite be set to zero, nor quite
erase knowledge to recover
a pure and isotropic field
stretching out towards a perfect horizon

And this is where you lose identity
on the edge of the ocean
hidden in stones from the river
where there is no daylight
just a weak beat tracking sidereal time
the scenery folds up
and the erasure of all discrete points
rolls light aside to reveal an equal array
dispersed over all parts of the sky
boundless and colourless

## Y1 Cold River 3

The rite rolls the river back and I cross dry-shod on horizontal willows
I walk out onto the far bank with empty arms
The bed of the river yields wrecks and branches of trees
The clay lies in coloured stripes.

The new life has stray sounds without tunes.
Cold turned all the rhythms off
the nearly erased becomes audible and stalks around as ghosts,
phrases that turn and never complete,
prosody without words. The conversation of objects.
The pivot that turns the cylinder of time itself rusts.
An empty terrain a featureless land

The river's gullet shapes pure cubes, spheres and cylinders of clay
elements of a city part inside and out
a maze clumsily scratched on the beach
the clay takes pigments and shape
for its outside.
For words I have clay toys with clay mouths
the model is about to become an abstraction
but is too dumb to arrive there.
Empty space pours itself out of a hole
too early for objects.
I start my life without rules
sinking to folk level and fixing stylised movements
in static forms, that don't break easily.
I take pebbles from the river bed
and set them out in patterns
I pour water on them to make them shine

## NOTES

A History of Shopping. I started this in 2003, left it alone, wrote most of it in 2018.

William Hallam Pegg. Based on lace designs by William Hallam Pegg (1864–1946), held in the lace archive at Nottingham Trent University, mainly the 1933 one on the breakdown of trade talks. The full title is 'Needlepoint Lace and Embroidery Panel recording the abortive economic conference of 64 nations in London 1933, with its concomitant Orgy of destruction'. Pegg was a communist and his design depicts the world through its bridges and monuments (one for each of 64 countries), to evoke hunger and the fruits of the earth.

The Dumb Book (= An Leabhar Balbh). John O'Donovan, in his 1844 translation of another Mac Fhirbhisigh's great corpus of genealogies, suggests that the *Leabhar balbh* was stories that the great families did not want told. It has now disappeared.

Wine and Pine Resin. This is a slightly tweaked output from the computer program GPT-2. Some of the 'feedstock' was my own poetry.

Torthorwald. This is a poem from a long time ago which was never collected. My ancestor led the parish out against the Jacobite army because James III was a Catholic. The story is in the 1848 *Life* of Henry Duncan.

'Controlled Conditions' is a poem from a book of 1981, of which about half was cut. But, I reprieved this one.

Capistranus Triumphans. The start was a sentence in Franz Babinger's *Mehmet the Conqueror* in which he says that Capistrano preached to crowds of twenty or thirty thousand even though they were quite unable to understand the language he preached in, Latin. Most of the details in the poem come from a 17th century Latin work, a life of Capistrano (by Amandus Herman) which runs to 800 pages.

Calendar Rite. Agon, "contest". The term refers to Roger Caillois' book on the Game. It is in this case a ritual contest.

Inside and Out: the title comes from a book of that name by Adrian Stokes, and the poem paraphrases another book of his, *Stones of Rimini*.

On the Origin of his Body: name of a 5$^{th}$ C text (*Peri tēs gennēs tou sōmatos autou*) identified as Mani's autobiography and known as the Cologne Mani Codex. 'Gofyn a diolch': the phrase means "request and thanks". The poet requests a lavish gift and then writes a thanks poem after receiving it. Both poems include lavish descriptions. Part of "Gofyn a diolch" is derived from a GPT-2 run.

'anything that has been alive will rot down' – a quote from Bob Flowerdew.

*Ich-Gestein*: title of a painting by Gerhard Altenbourg, a dissident painter in East Germany. The phrase means "self-mineral".

ACKNOWLEDGEMENTS

The following poems have been published in magazines. My warm thanks go to Tony Frazer, Gisele Parnall, and David Caddy, the editors concerned. 'Who owns the water', 'Llyn Cerrig Bach' and 'Equidistant' were published in *Tears in the Fence*. 'The Brig at Torthorwald' was in *Shearsman* in 1996. 'Leabhar Balbh' was in *Shearsman*, issue 121/122. 'A Route March in the Cultural Field' was in *Naviformes*, #1.

www.ingramcontent.com/pod-product-compliance
Lightning Source LLC
Chambersburg PA
CBHW031637160426
43196CB00006B/454